Enrichment

READING

Peggy Kaye

Dear Student,

Here is your very own *Enrichment Reading* book. The book is filled with exciting reading things to do at home. In it you will find games, contests, puzzles, riddles, information, stories, and all sorts of surprises. Best of all, you may ask your family or friends to work on the activities with you.

While you are having fun, you will be doing a lot of reading. You will also be learning how exciting reading can be.

Your friends at *Enrichment Reading* hope this book will be one of your favorite things to do. Good luck and happy reading!

Enrichment Series Copyright © 1991 SRA/McGraw-Hill

Contents

Hidden Crickets

A fact about crickets is hiding in this puzzle.

i	e	a		c	o	r	i	a	e
c	e	a	k	a	e	e	t		h
o	e	a	i	r	s		a	w	i
i	e	i	t	h		i	a	t	o
e	s		e	l	e	e	g	s	

Write the missing letters in the twelve words below.
Do the words in order.
Color the boxes in the puzzle that have the letters you wrote.
Follow the same order you used to write the letters.
You will skip over many letters in the puzzle.

1. k ___ t ___

2. b ___ ___ t

3. p ___ n

4. l ___ ___ f

5. c ___ n ___

6. p ___ t

7. r ___ p

8. n ___ ___ l

9. t ___ ___

10. h ___ t

11. r ___ s ___

12. b ___ ___ t

Now write the letters you did not color in order.

___ ___ ___ ___ ___ ___ ___ ___ ___ ___ ___ ___

___ ___ ___ ___ ___ ___ ___ ___ ___ ___ ___ .

Word Road

Play this game with an adult or a friend.
Get a small marker for each player.
A paper clip and a button will do.
Put both markers on GO.
Take turns. Toss two pennies onto a table or the floor.
If they land with two heads up, move 3 spaces on the Word Road.
If they land with two tails up, move 2 spaces.
If they land with one tail and one head up, move 1 space.
Read the word you land on.
If you land on a word with a long vowel, stay in that space.
If you land on a word with a short vowel, go back 2 spaces.
The first player to get HOME wins the game.

2 heads = 3 spaces
2 tails = 2 spaces
1 head and 1 tail = 1 space

Word Road

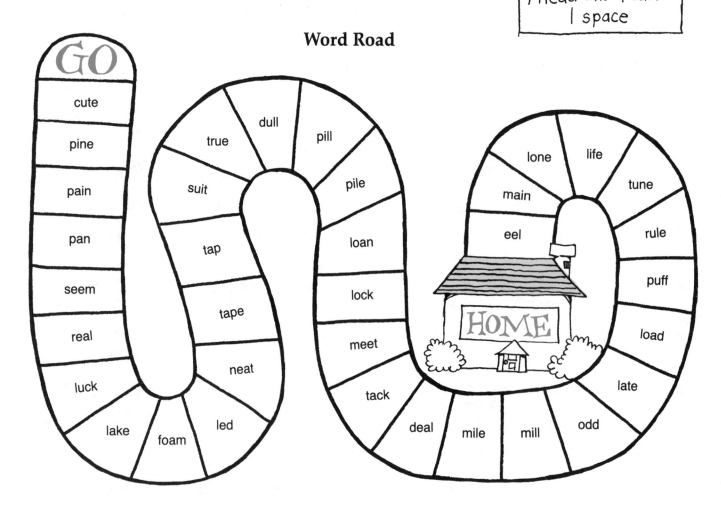

Who won? _____

2 ▶ Points for Words

Here are four word wheels.
Four word parts are on each wheel.
Add one or more letters to finish each word.
Score 5 points for every word you make.
Write your score on a piece of paper after you finish each wheel.
Try to get at least 60 points.

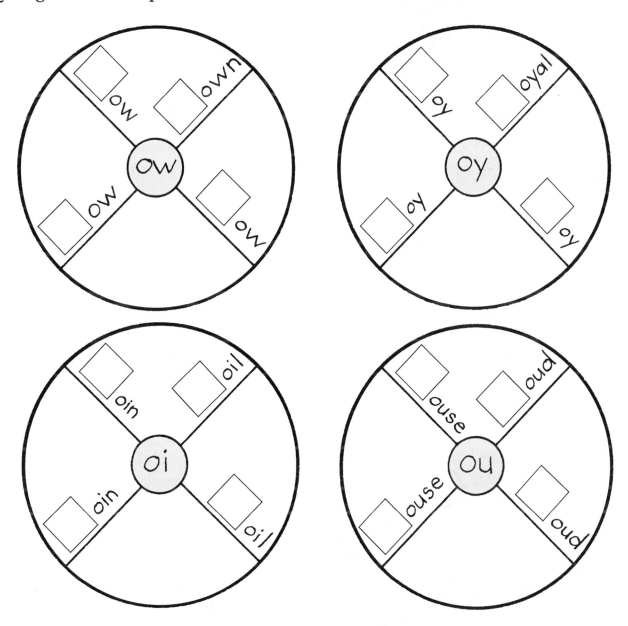

How many points did you get? _____

Break the Bank

Play this game with a friend.
Take turns.
Toss something small onto the playing board.
Look at the word part where your marker landed.
Try to make a word by adding one or more letters
from your letter bank to the word part.
You may also use other letters.
Write your word on a sheet of paper.
Cross out any letters you use from your Letter Bank.
You win if you cross out all the letters in your bank first.

My Letter Bank
f l l d b p
t c n n t h

My Friend's Letter Bank
f l l d b p
t c n n t h

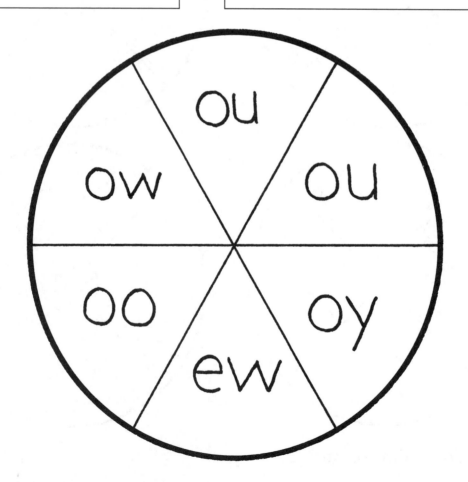

③ ▶ Word Explosion

There has been a word explosion.
Ten words have been blown apart.
Help the frog and owl put the words back together.
Connect all the words you can.
One has been done for you.

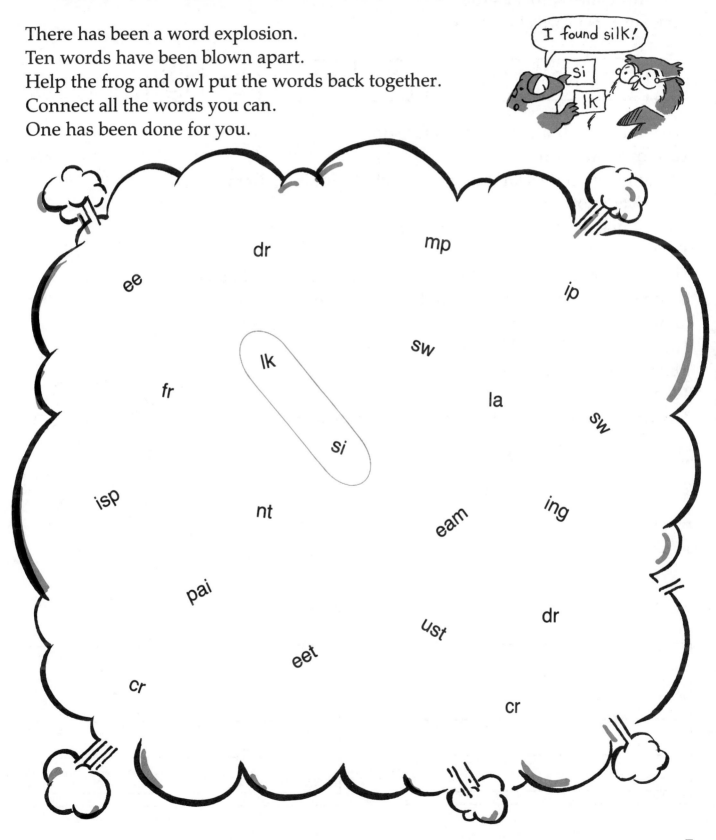

Make a Word

Play this game with an adult.
Make number cards like these.

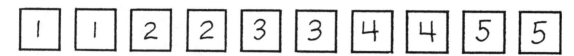

Mix up the cards and turn them face down.
Turn over one card.
The number on the card tells you which beginning letters to use.
Turn over another card.
The number on the card tells you which middle letter to use.
Turn over a third card.
The number on the card tells you which ending letters to use.
If you can use the beginning, middle, and ending letters
to make a real word, write the word on your Word Card.
Turn your cards face down after you use them.
Mix up all the cards again.
Take turns.
The first player to make three words wins the game.

Beginning	Middle	Ending
1. st	**1.** a	**1.** ck
2. cr	**2.** e	**2.** nd
3. bl	**3.** i	**3.** st
4. ch	**4.** o	**4.** mp
5. cl	**5.** u	**5.** sh

My Word Card	My Adult's Word Card
_____	_____
_____	_____
_____	_____

Name _____

 4 Odd Names

Tom Henderson decided to mix up his name.
First he wrote down all the word parts, or **syllables**, in his name.

tom   hen   der   son

Then he mixed up the syllables.

hen   son   tom   der

Finally he blended the syllables together into one word.

Hensontomder

What an odd name!

Now turn your name into an odd name.
Write your name here.

_____

Write all the syllables here.

_____

Mix up the syllables.

_____

Put them together into an odd name.

_____

Use the name of a friend to make another odd name.
Write the name here.

_____

Write all the syllables here.

_____

Mix up the syllables.

_____

Put them together into an odd name.

_____

On another sheet of paper, make up three more odd names.

The Great Mix-up

Try to turn mixed-up words into real words.
Give this page to an adult.
Have your adult read one of the mixed-up words to you.
Listen carefully.
Then try to switch the syllables until you can say a real word.
If you can say a real word, the adult colors a star for you.
Then go on to a new word.

tersis ?

1. tersis   (sister)

2. bowrain   (rainbow)

3. mintperpep   (peppermint)

4. scrapersky   (skyscraper)

5. antgi   (giant)

6. akeetpar   (parakeet)

7. derspi   (spider)

8. gerti   (tiger)

9. tapoto   (potato)

10. shotsling   (slingshot)

11. hopgrassper   (grasshopper)

12. ballfoot   (football)

13. appineple   (pineapple)

14. cubercum   (cucumber)

How many colored stars did you earn? _____

Name _____

How much do you know about bees?
Read each question.
To find the right answer, circle the correct plural
for the word in dark print.
The right answer is above the correct plural.

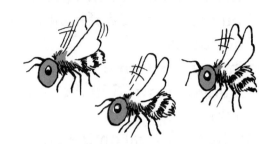

1. About how many flowers does it take to make a pound of honey?

	2,000	20,000	2,000,000
chair	chairys	chaires	chairs

2. What makes a bee's buzzing sound?

	its mouth	its wings	its legs
peach	peachs	peaches	peachess

3. Which is the only kind of bee that dies after it stings?

	a bumblebee	a killer bee	a honeybee
leaf	leafs	leafes	leaves

4. How many eggs does a queen honeybee lay in a day?

	1,500	100	15
berry	berries	berrys	berryes

5. Where does a honeybee turn nectar into honey?

	in its mouth	in its honey stomach	in small bags under its mouth
body	bodys	bodies	bodyes

Circle the number that tells how many of the bee

facts surprised you.   1   2   3   4   5

Color Three

This is a game for two players.
You each need a different color crayon.
Take turns.
Choose a box on the Color Three Board.
Change the word in the box from the singular
to the plural.
Write the plural on the line.
If both players agree the plural is correct, color the box.
The first player to color three boxes in a row is the winner.
The row may go up and down, across, or on a slant.

Color Three Board

shelf _____	daisy _____	slice _____
elbow _____	ash _____	child _____
bakery _____	task _____	speech _____

6 Star Lines

You can make a very big star.
Find three forms of the same word around the circle.
Use a ruler to draw straight lines to connect the words.
Keep on connecting words until the star is finished.
Then color the star.

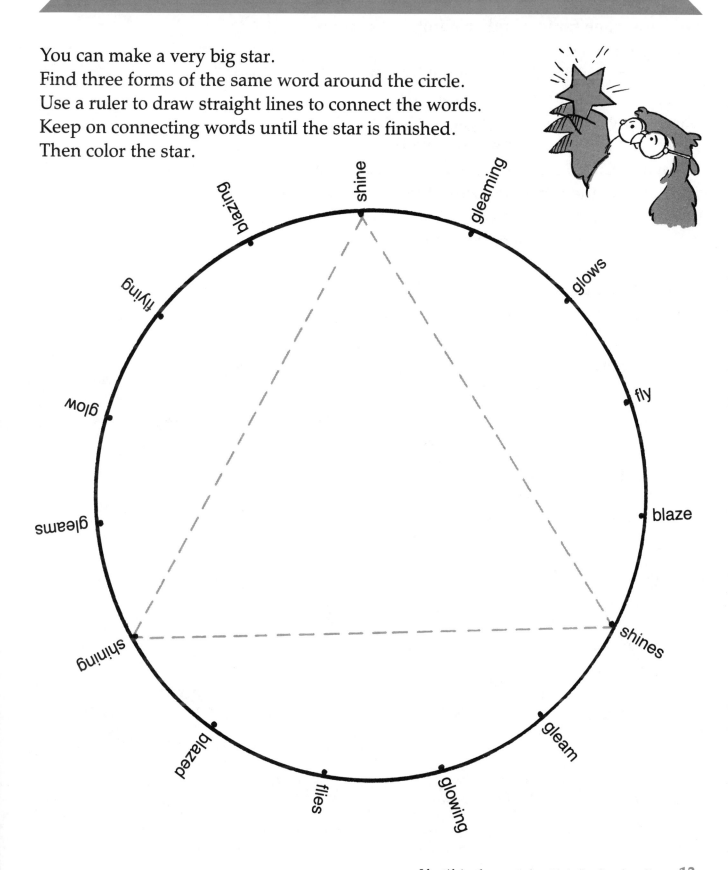

Word Collector

Here is a game for you and an adult.

Toss a penny.

If the penny lands tails up, you lose the turn.

If it lands heads up, you collect words.

Choose any word on the page and cross it out.

Then hunt for other forms of the word.

You may want to turn the page around as you look.

Cross out all the different forms of the word you can find.

Write all the words you cross out on a sheet of paper.

If you miss a word, you or your partner will collect it later.

Take turns.

Keep playing until all the words are crossed out.

The person who collects more words wins the game.

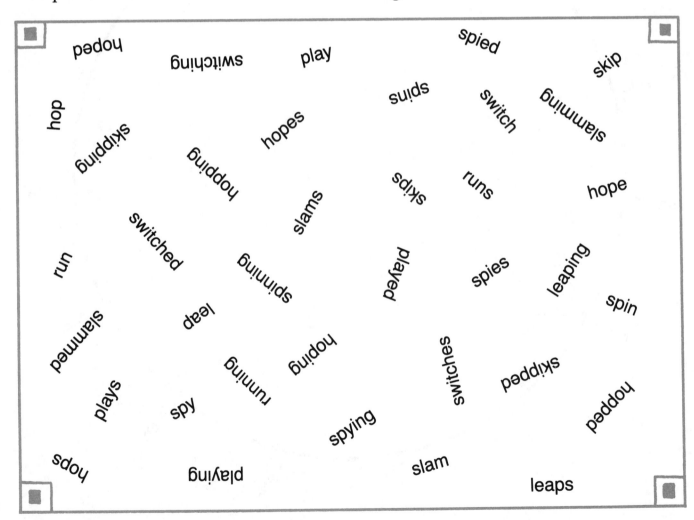

Name _____

Silly Compounds

Read each pair of words at the right.
Say each pair as a regular compound.
The first pair would be **teapot.**
Now make silly compounds by joining the words in
different ways.
Join **dog** and **fly** to make **dogfly**.
Write the silly compound dogfly on the line in box **1** below.
Draw a picture in the box to match your idea of a dogfly.
Write a new silly compound in each of the other boxes.
Draw pictures to match your ideas of the silly compounds.

tea	pot
butter	fly
rain	coat
dog	house
sail	boat
paint	brush

My Silly Compounds

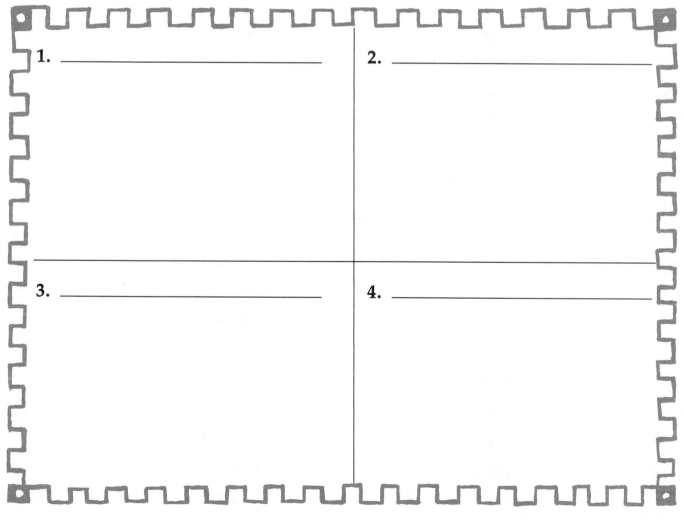

1. _____   2. _____

3. _____   4. _____

Contraction Race

Play this game with a friend.
One player takes the top of the page.
The other player takes the bottom.
Say GO and start drawing lines to connect contractions
with the words that make them up.
The first player to finish says STOP.
If all of that player's lines are correct, the player wins.
If there are mistakes, the player must erase the errors.
Then someone says GO again, and the game continues.
The winner is the first player to match correctly all the words.

you have	won't
who is	you'd
we have	you're
does not	wouldn't
it will	you've
would not	doesn't
will not	who's
you would	it'll
you are	we've

we've	you are
it'll	you would
who's	will not
doesn't	would not
you've	it will
wouldn't	does not
you're	we have
you'd	who is
won't	you have

Name _____

What is hiding in this picture?
Connect the words in alphabetical order to find out.
Sometimes two words start with the same letter.
Then look at the second letter before connecting the words.

mice

jack

no

add

wax   not

in

be

team

by

so

cow

eel

race

ice

fly

pen

hop

go

What did you find hiding in the picture? _____

Alphabet Code

Do this activity with an adult.
You can write words in code by putting the letters in alphabetical order.
If your name is Paul, you become Alpu.
Samantha becomes Aaahmnst.

Try it with your name.

Your name   Your name in code

_____   _____

Let your adult try.

Your adult's name   Your adult's name in code

_____   _____

Choose three more words.
They should not be more than five letters long.
Rewrite each word with its letters in alphabetical order.
Give the page to your adult.
Can your adult figure out your words?

My words in code   Did your adult figure out the word?

_____   YES   NO

_____   YES   NO

_____   YES   NO

Now let your adult write words in code.
You try to figure them out.

My adult's words in code   Did you figure out the word?

_____   YES   NO

_____   YES   NO

_____   YES   NO

⑨ Dictionary Mystery

Here are six dictionary entries.
There are pronunciations.
There are the definitions.
There are sample sentences.
The only things missing are the entry words.
Try to add the correct entry words.
Be sure to spell each entry word correctly.

Entry word

_____

(rōz)
A flower that grows on bushes
and vines.
The red rose smells sweet.

Entry word

_____

(rab′it)
A small animal that has
long ears.
My rabbit can hop.

Entry word

_____

(foks)
A wild animal that lives in
the woods.
The fox hunts for its food.

Entry word

_____

(pē an′ō)
A musical instrument that
has many keys.
I take piano lessons.

Entry word

_____

(lāk)
A body of water that is
surrounded by land.
Let's go swimming in the lake.

Entry word

_____

(bās′bôl′)
A game played with a bat
and a ball.
I am on a baseball team.

Dictionary Numbers

Do this activity with an adult.
Make number cards like these.

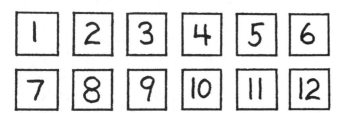

Turn the cards face down and mix them up.
Now read the four dictionary entries below.
Each entry has a pronunciation, a definition, and
a sample sentence.
Choose an entry and look at the numbers in front of
its three parts.
Next, pick three number cards.
If your cards have the same numbers as your entry,
you are a winner.
If your cards do not have the same numbers, return
one of your cards face down.
Mix up the cards again.
Give your adult a turn.
On your next turn, pick one new card and see if you
are a winner now.
Take turns trading in cards until someone is a winner.

pen guin
10 (pen′gwin)
 6 An animal that lives
   in or near Antarctica.
 1 *A penguin is black and
   white.*

pup py
12 (pup′ē)
 4 A young dog.
 5 *The puppy barked.*

por cu pine
 2 (pôr′kyə pīn)
 3 An animal whose body is
   covered with quills.
11 *The porcupine lives in
   the woods.*

py thon
 9 (pī′thon)
 8 A large snake.
 7 *I saw a python at the zoo.*

Name _____

Read the silly poem below and then rewrite it.
Change every underlined word into an opposite.

In the <u>beautiful</u> land of Goop-dee-goo
  <u>Everyone</u> eats a <u>sweet</u> apple stew.
The <u>boys</u> <u>walk</u> <u>backwards</u> all day long
  And <u>whisper</u> when they sing a song.
The <u>girls</u> are always kind and fair.
  They have <u>big</u> thumbs and <u>long</u> green hair.
It <u>never</u> rains, so <u>remember</u> that—
  You <u>won't</u> need an umbrella or a hat.
Please <u>come</u> along <u>here</u> to Goop-dee-goo,
  We'll all be looking <u>out</u> for you.
                            Peggy Kaye

Rewrite the poem here.

_____

_____

_____

_____

_____

_____

_____

_____

_____

Read the new poem you made.
Which poem do you think is sillier? Circle your answer.   Poem 1   Poem 2

Go Fish

Play this game with an adult.
Make eighteen word cards like these.

quick	fast	slow	friend	cold	enemy
nice	mean	kind	bright	shiny	dull
chilly	pal	hot	easy	hard	simple

Mix up the cards.
Deal four cards to each player.
Spread the rest of the cards face down for a fish pile.
Try for a match of three cards in your hand.
A match must have <u>two</u> cards with words that
mean the same thing (**fast, quick**) and
<u>one</u> card that means the opposite (**slow**).
If you did not have a match from
the deal, ask your adult for a card
that will help you make one.
Your adult must give you any card
that will help you make a match.
Then you may ask for another card.
If your adult does not have a matching
card, she or he says, "Go fish."
You select a card from the fish pile
and then your turn ends.
Now your adult can ask you for a card.
As soon as a player has three matching
cards, they are put on the table and
the player reads the words aloud.
Play until all the cards are matched.
The player with more matches is the winner.

Do you have a match for **cold**?

Yes, I have **hot** and **chilly**.

11 ▸ Which Word?

The sun and its planets move through the Milky Way.
Do you know how fast the sun and planets are moving?
To find out, write the correct word in each sentence.
Look at the number next to the word you chose.
Write that number in the Number Box.
Start at the left and do not skip any spaces.
Add up all the numbers you wrote and
put the sum on the last line in the box.

Come over _____.	hear **10**	here **20**
The wind _____ all night.	blew **25**	blue **15**
I can _____ you.	see **25**	sea **10**
That mouse has a long _____.	tail **15**	tale **10**
We _____ the race!	one **15**	won **30**
Look at my _____ bike.	knew **20**	new **25**
How much does a whale _____?	weigh **20**	way **15**
Put the belt on your _____.	waste **10**	waist **15**

Number Box

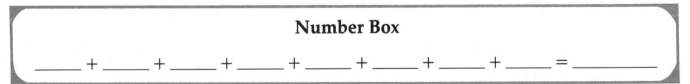

Complete this sentence with the sum from the Number Box.

The sun and planets travel _____ miles every second!

Riddle Time

This activity is for you and an adult.
Try to answer this riddle.
  What is a pony with a cold?
  Answer: It is a **hoarse horse**, of course.
How good is your adult at solving riddles?
Read the riddles below to your adult.
Let the adult try to solve each riddle.
Tell your adult that every answer has two words that sound exactly alike.
Circle YES when your adult can solve a riddle.
Circle NO when your adult cannot think of the answer.
You will find the answer below each riddle.

1. What do you call a tired red vegetable?   YES   NO
   Answer   a beat beet

2. What is a simple jetliner?   YES   NO
   Answer   a plain plane

3. What do you call bargain days at a boat store?   YES   NO
   Answer   a sail sale

4. What is a charming woodland animal?   YES   NO
   Answer   a dear deer

5. What do you need to make rose and daisy cake?   YES   NO
   Answer   flower flour

6. What do you call a person who sells basements?   YES   NO
   Answer   a cellar seller

7. What do you call a bit of rabbit fur?   YES   NO
   Answer   hare hair

8. What do you call a light-colored bucket?   YES   NO
   Answer   a pale pail

12 ▶ Word Puzzle

There are two sentences for each word that goes
in the puzzle below.
Try to think of one word that fits both sentences.
Write that word in the puzzle, one letter to a box.

Across

2. You _____ go to the show.
My birthday is on _____ 11th.

3. I _____ a blue bird.
I will _____ the wood.

4. Do not _____ the bus.
My teacher is _____ Jones.

5. _____ me the book.
Look at the clock's big _____.

8. You have dirt on your _____.
A clock has hands and a _____.

9. I will act in a _____.
I want to _____ baseball.

Down

1. Turn on the _____.
The bag feels _____.

2. I know what you _____.
Be nice! Don't be _____.

6. I will _____ the cards.
It is a fair _____.

7. They _____ 1 hour ago.
It is in my _____ hand.

8. The bird can _____.
Don't let the _____ in
the house.

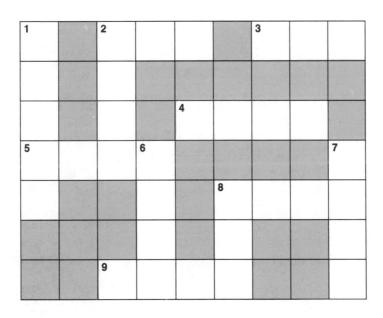

Two Meanings

Do this activity with a friend.
Choose one of the words listed below.
Try to use the word twice in a single sentence.
The sentence must show two different meanings of the word.
Tell your friend your sentence.
Take turns choosing words and making up sentences until
you finish the list.
Write your name next to the words you try.
Circle YES if you can make the sentence.
Circle NO if you cannot make the sentence.

Word	Who tried the word?	Did you make a sentence?	
bark	_____	YES	NO
leave	_____	YES	NO
ball	_____	YES	NO
case	_____	YES	NO
duck	_____	YES	NO
jam	_____	YES	NO
fan	_____	YES	NO
mine	_____	YES	NO
fall	_____	YES	NO

13 ▶ The Wrong Words

Read this story about a lion and a mouse.
As you read, you will find nine words that do not belong.
Write the words in order at the bottom of the page.

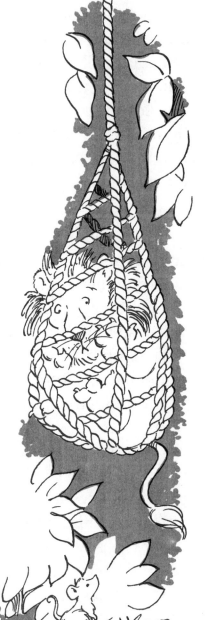

One day in the jungle, a big lion grabbed a little mouse. The lion held the mouse in his paws.

The mouse looked up at the lion and your said, "Please let me go. I am too little to be a good meal. And if you heart let me go, someday I will help you."

The lion laughed, "You help beats me! What a silly idea." The lion one laughed so hard, that it let the mouse slip away. The mouse ran home.

Several weeks hundred passed by. The mouse was at home fixing thousand dinner for his wife. Suddenly, he heard the lion roaring in pain. The mouse ran from his house. He ran through the times woods. He found the lion stuck in a rope trap. The lion every pulled at the ropes, but couldn't get free.

The mouse said, "I'll save you, friend lion."

The little mouse started chewing on the ropes. Soon one rope had a big hole in it. Then another rope had a hole. Then another and another. In a few minutes, the lion was day free. The lion smiled at the mouse and said, "You are little, but you saved the king of the beasts. Thank you, my special friend."

This is a fact. _____ _____ _____

_____ _____ _____ _____

_____ _____!

What's Next?

Give this page to an adult.
Have the adult read you this story about the inventor Thomas Edison.
You may not look at the page.
Some words in the story are underlined.
The adult will stop reading just before saying an underlined word.
You try to guess what word comes next.
You score 2 points if you guess the word.
If you cannot guess, the adult tells you the first letter of the word.
If you can guess the word now, you score 1 point.
Keep score on a piece of paper.

When Thomas Edison was four years <u>old</u>, he was curious about why the family goose spent the entire day sitting on her eggs. His mother explained that a <u>goose</u> sits on her eggs to keep them <u>warm</u>. The eggs must stay warm so that they will <u>hatch</u>.

That afternoon, Tom went out to the barn. Many hours passed. Tom's parents and sister began to worry. What could Tom be doing in the <u>barn</u>? They went to find out.

What do you think they saw? There was Tom curled up in the <u>nest</u>. Tom's father said, "Tom, why are you sitting in a goose nest?"

"I'm hatching eggs," Tom answered.

Tom's sister laughed. "Don't you know anything? You can't hatch <u>eggs</u>."

Tom stood <u>up</u>. Then he saw something. All the eggs were <u>crushed</u>. Tom looked at himself. He was completely covered <u>with</u> yolk. Tom began to <u>cry</u>. That was Thomas Edison's very first experiment.

The highest possible score is 20 points.

How many points did you score? _____

Name _____

Think of all the people you know.
Think of friends and relatives.
Think of characters from books, movies, and TV.
Try to think of just the right person
for each sentence below.
When you have the right person in mind,
write the person's name on the blank line.

1. _____ runs as fast as a cheetah.

2. _____ has a voice like a police siren.

3. _____ plays like a silly kitten.

4. _____ can be as quiet as a pillow.

5. _____ is as strong as a polar bear.

6. _____ is as smart as an encyclopedia.

7. _____ is as friendly as a puppy greeting its master.

8. _____ can get as nervous as a rabbit.

9. _____ dresses in colors like a rainbow.

10. _____ can be as sneaky as a fox.

A Monster Story

Have a friend do this activity with you.
Fill in each blank in the story.
You may take turns or work together.
Use words from the Word Box or your own words.

The Monster

A monster just moved in next door. The monster is

nice, but it is as tall as a _____

with hair as green as _____, eyes as

yellow as _____, and skin that feels

like _____. Its voice sounds like

_____.

The monster cooks special food that looks like

_____ and smells like

_____. When the monster is eating,

it sounds like _____.

Yesterday the monster invited me over to play. It

has a ball that is as big as a _____

and a bat that looks like a _____.

I picked up the bat, but it felt as heavy as a

_____. I said, "Let's draw

pictures instead." The monster agreed, so I drew a

picture of the monster, and the monster drew a

picture of me.

You and your friend draw pictures of the monster.
Use separate sheets of paper for your pictures.

Word Box

baby
beach ball
building
crashing cars
crayon
earthquakes
fence posts
fire alarms
frog
gorilla
hay
rotten eggs
house
leaves
mountain
sandpaper
silk
street light
the sun
tree
thunder

Name _____

Think of three words that have to do with the word <u>circus</u>.
Write them on these lines.

_____   _____

_____

Choose one of your three words.
Write it in box **A** at the right.

A

Write three other words that go with the word in box **A**.

_____   _____

_____

Choose a word from your second list.
Write it in box **B** at the right.

B

Write three other words that go with the word in box **B**.
Do not use any words you used before.

_____   _____

_____

Choose a word from your third list.
Write it in box **C** at the right.

C

Write three other words that go with the word in box **C**.
Do not use any words you used before.

_____   _____

_____

Look at all the words you wrote.
Try to make a sentence using at least one word
from each of your lists.

_____

_____

Shared Thinking

Have a friend do this activity with you.

For **Round 1**, you and your friend think of the word <u>baseball</u>.

Do not talk to each other.

On this page, write six baseball words that come into your mind.

Your friend writes six words on another sheet of paper.

Do not show each other your papers until you are finished.

When you both are finished, compare your lists.

Score 1 point for every word that is on both lists.

Each of you write your score at the bottom of your own list.

Play **Round 2** for <u>school</u> and **Round 3** for <u>Halloween</u> in the same way.

Round 1 Baseball	**Round 2** School	**Round 3** Halloween
_____	_____	_____
_____	_____	_____
_____	_____	_____
_____	_____	_____
_____	_____	_____
_____	_____	_____
Score _____	**Score** _____	**Score** _____

How many points did you score in all? _____

Eleven to 18 points means you and your friend have thoughts that agree nearly perfectly.

Five to 10 points means you and your friend almost always think alike.

One to 4 points means you and your friend have ideas that are sometimes alike.

Zero means you and your friend are on different wavelengths.

You can do this activity again with three new words or with another partner.

Name _____

16 ▶ Class Partners

Welcome to Animal School.
Everyone in Animal School must have a partner.
Here is how to find yours.

   The animals in this class are in two groups.
   Read all the signs in both groups.
   Signs in **Group A** are sentence beginnings.
   Signs in **Group B** are sentence endings.
   Try to match each sentence beginning with its correct ending.
   Draw lines between the matching signs.
   When you are finished, the one animal in Group A without
a sentence ending will be your partner for the day.

Group A   **Group B**

Red is to stop

Car is to road

Hit is to baseball

Read is to book

Rain is to drop

Apple is to tree

as train is to track.

as green is to go.

as kick is to football.

as listen is to radio.

as eggs are to hens.

Who is your class partner for the day? _____

The Right Words

This is a game to play with a friend.
Here are twenty-one words.
Choose eight words for yourself and underline them.
Have your friend choose eight different words and circle them.

table	snow	foot	winter	bowl	hot	fire
paper	lane	clown	mouse	tiger	clock	milk
rink	nose	button	book	circle	spoon	electricity

Work with your friend to complete the sentences below.
You score 1 point every time you use an underlined word.
Your friend scores 1 point every time you use a circled word.
Keep track of your points on another sheet of paper.

Chalk is to board as pencil is to _____.

Glove is to hand as shoe is to _____.

August is to summer as January is to _____.

Swimming is to pool as ice-skating is to _____.

Milk is to glass as soup is to _____.

Ice is to cold as steam is to _____.

Sheep is to wool as cow is to _____.

Cars are to gas as lamps are to _____.

Baseball is to field as bowling is to _____.

Shoe is to lace as coat is to _____.

How many points did you score? _____

How many points did your friend score? _____

Name _____

Pam and Kana entered a writing contest.
Each hopes that her paragraph is the best.
You be the judge.
Read each paragraph.
Remember a good paragraph has one main idea.
All the sentences in the paragraph should be
filled with information about that idea.

Pam's Paragraph

A volcano is an opening in the earth. When the earth
opens, gas and rock shoot up into the air from deep
inside the earth. I have never seen a volcano. The rock is
melted. It has a special name. My nickname is Pammy.
The rock is called magma. When magma comes out of
the volcano it is called lava.

Kana's Paragraph

When the lava hardens it becomes rocks. There are
many kinds of lava rocks. A block is a lava rock with
sharp corners. A bomb is a round piece of lava rock. A
cinder is a very light rock. The lightest lava rock of all is
called pumice. Pumice rock is so light it floats on water.

Who should win the first prize ribbon? _____

What is the main idea of the first prize paragraph?

_____

_____

_____

_____

Identifying the main idea   **35**

Sentence Match

Play this game with a friend.

At the bottom of the page are two main ideas for a paragraph, one for you and one for a friend.

You must match your main idea with sentences from the Sentence List.

Make number cards like those at the right.

Mix up the cards and turn them face down.

Take turns picking a card.

The card you pick tells you which sentence you get from the list.

If the sentence matches your main idea, write the number under your main idea.

If it does not, put the card back.

The winner is the first player to match four sentences to his or her main idea.

| 1 | 2 | 3 | 4 |
| 5 | 6 | 7 | 8 |

Sentence List

1. An elephant's trunk is also its nose.
2. Giraffes are so tall, they can see enemies from far away.
3. Its skin color helps it to hide in the trees and grass.
4. There is a finger on the end of the nose.
5. The nose is so strong it can pull down trees.
6. It can kick an enemy with its long legs.
7. To take a shower, an elephant fills its nose with water.
8. It can hit an enemy with its strong neck.

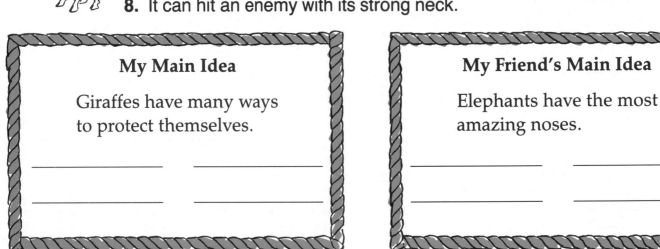

My Main Idea

Giraffes have many ways to protect themselves.

_____ _____

_____ _____

My Friend's Main Idea

Elephants have the most amazing noses.

_____ _____

_____ _____

Name _____

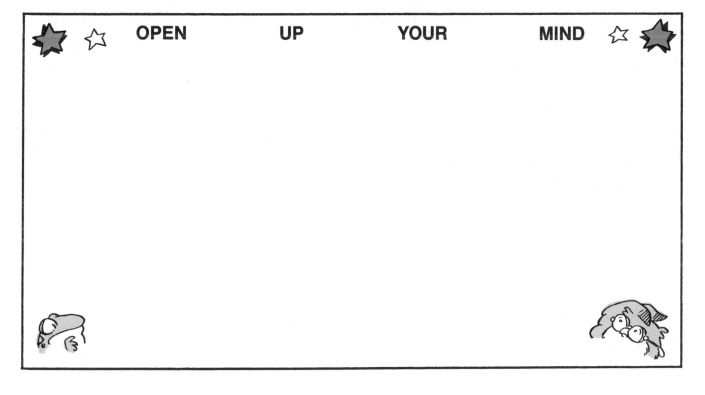

★ ☆ **OPEN   UP   YOUR   MIND** ☆ ★

Follow the directions below.
You will OPEN UP YOUR MIND to another message.
Each time you change a letter or letters in a word,
rewrite the new spelling below the word that is changed.

1. Switch P and N in the first word.

2. Change all the vowels in the last two words to O.

3. Change the first and last letters of the whole message to K.

4. Change M to W.

5. Add the word THE between the second and third words.

6. Change R to D.

7. Change the first N to E and the last N to R.

8. Change Y to G.

Write your new message here.

_____ _____ _____ _____ _____

Do As I Say

Ask a friend to play this game.
Choose one of the sets of instructions below.
Read the instructions to your friend.
When you finish reading, have your friend try to follow the
instructions in order without looking at the page.
If your friend follows them correctly, write his or her name in the box.
If your friend cannot follow them, leave the box blank.
Then have your friend choose a set of instructions for you to follow.
Keep playing until you have names in all six boxes.

Set 1
Stand up.
Touch your toes three times.
Turn around.
Shout, "Hello!"

_____

Set 4
Sit on the floor.
Clap your hands once.
Rub your tummy.
Pull on your ears.

_____

Set 2
Skip to the nearest door.
Knock on the door.
Say, "Surprise!"
Jump up in the air.

_____

Set 5
Make a silly face.
Say, "Banana, banana."
Touch your nose with
your thumb.

_____

Set 3
Hum a tune.
Put both hands in the air.
Growl like a dog.
Blink your eyes three times.

_____

Set 6
Touch one knee with both hands.
Jump two times.
Say, "I'm hungry!"
Stamp your feet.

_____

Name _____

Here are menus from three different restaurants.
One restaurant is for monsters. It is called Monster Cafe.
One restaurant is for babies. It is called Baby Bits.
One restaurant is for sports stars. It is called Fitness Food.
The restaurants' names are missing from the menus.
Read each menu. Write the restaurant's name at the top.
Then add today's special dish at the bottom.

First course
Mashed banana
Applesauce

Main course
Little bits of hamburger
Mashed potatoes

Dessert
Warm milk in a bottle
Pudding

Today's special

_____

_____

First course
Worm dumpling
Eye of bat soup

Main course
Spider stew
Fried lion's paw

Dessert
Paste and dirt pie
Twig and leaf cake

Today's special

_____

_____

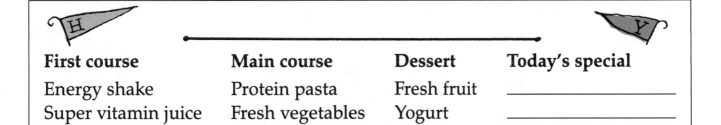

First course	**Main course**	**Dessert**	**Today's special**
Energy shake	Protein pasta	Fresh fruit	_____
Super vitamin juice	Fresh vegetables	Yogurt	_____

What Is My Job?

Play this game with an adult.
Look at the lists of jobs below.
Pick one of them or choose any other job you want.
Do not tell your adult which one you chose.
Tell three things about the job, but do not give its name.
Here is an example.

    You come to me when you are hungry.
    I sell fruits, vegetables, and other kinds of food.
    When you finish visiting me, you go home with
    a bag full of good things to eat.
    What is my job?
If your adult can guess the job, score 1 point.
Take turns.
Play three rounds and keep score in the Score Box.

JOBS

a cook	a carpenter	a ballet dancer
a doctor	a bank teller	an animal trainer
a plumber	a fire fighter	a pet store owner
a teacher	a mail carrier	a shoe salesperson
a musician	a window washer	a newspaper reporter

Score Box	
Me	**My Adult**
Round 1	Round 1
Round 2	Round 2
Round 3	Round 3
Total	Total

20 ▸ What Will Happen?

Here is part of a story about Julian who has a loose tooth.

"Well," my father said, "if you wait long enough, it will fall out." He was talking about my tooth, my right bottom front tooth.

"How long do I have to wait?" I asked. Because I had *two* right bottom front teeth—one firm little new one pushing in, and one wiggly old one.

"I can't say," my father said. "Maybe a month, maybe two months. Maybe less."

"I don't want to wait," I said. "I want *one* tooth there, and I don't want to wait two months!"

"All right!" said my father. "I'll take care of it!" He jumped out of his chair and ran out the door to the garage. He was back in a minute, carrying something—a pair of pliers!

"Your tooth is a little loose already," my father said. "So I'll just put the pliers in your mouth for a second, twist, and the tooth will come out. You won't feel a thing!"

"I won't feel a thing?" I looked at the pliers—huge, black-handled pliers with a long pointed tip. I thought I *would* feel a thing. I thought it would hurt.

"Shall I?" said my dad. He raised the pliers toward my mouth.

What do you think will happen next?
Write your ideas here or on another sheet of paper.

_____

_____

Do you want to know what really happens?
You can find out in the book *The Stories Julian Tells* by Ann Cameron.

Problems, Problems

Ask an adult to work on these problems with you.

My Problems

Read this problem to yourself.

You are in a food store. You want to pay for the food, but you forgot your money at home. What do you do?

Read these three plans.
Underline the plan that tells what you would do.

1. Go home and get money.
2. Ask the storekeeper to wait for the money.
3. Phone a friend to bring money.

Now read the same problem and plans to your adult.
Circle the choice your adult picks.

Read this problem to yourself.

Your favorite TV show is on, but your TV is not working. What do you do?

Read these three plans.
Underline the plan that tells what you would do.

1. Forget the show for tonight.
2. Visit a friend and watch the show there.
3. Try to fix the TV.

Now read the same problem and plans to your adult.
Circle the choice your adult picks.

My Adult's Problem

Let your adult have a turn reading this problem and its plans with you.

You are rushing to get ready for school and juice spills on your homework. What do you do?

1. Give the teacher the homework with juice stains on it.
2. Redo the homework before school starts.
3. Leave the homework at home and tell the teacher what happened.

Now write the number of the plan that tells what you would do. _____

My adult thought I would pick plan number _____.

Name _____

21 ▸ Crime Buster

Mrs. Glow's biggest diamond is missing.
Here are four police reports.
Read each one.
Then fill in the Crime Buster Sheet.

Police Log Captain Smith

8:15 PM - Mrs. Glow called to report
a stolen diamond. Three diamond
thieves are in town - Diamond Bugs,
Diamond Stan, and Unlucky Lou. I
sent Detectives Shin, Gomez, and
Foster to investigate.

Police Log Detective Shin

7:30 PM - Last time Mrs. Glow saw
the diamond.
7:50 PM - Butler heard noises in
Mrs. Glow's room.
8:00 PM - Cook saw a red car
speeding away from house.

Police Log Detective Foster

Bugs and Stan drive red cars.
Lou has a blue car.
7:00 - 8:30 PM - Bugs had dinner
at the Drippy Diner and then
left.
8:30 PM - Lou walked in and took
a seat.

Police Log Detective Gomez

4:00 PM - Stan went to store to buy a
present for his wife's birthday.
4:30 - 9:30 PM - Stan was at wife's party.
5:00 PM - Lou borrowed Stan's car.
10:00 PM - Lou returned Stan's car
and gave flowers to Stan's wife.

Crime Buster Sheet

1. What time was the robbery? _____

2. What color car was the robber driving? _____

3. Who has that color car? _____

4. What was Bugs doing at the time of the robbery? _____

5. What was Stan doing at the time of the robbery? _____

6. Who was driving Stan's car? _____

7. What was Lou doing? _____

8. Whom should Police Captain Smith arrest? _____

Pyramids

Do this with a friend.

How was a pyramid built by the Egyptians of long ago?

It was hard work, and it took many years.

Here are four different pyramid building plans.

Only one plan gives the correct order for building a pyramid.

Read each plan.

Decide which plan is in correct order.

1. The land is measured.
   The desert is cleared.
   The pointed stone is set on top.
   The stones are put in place.
   The stones are polished.

2. The desert is cleared.
   The land is measured.
   The stones are put in place.
   The pointed stone is set on top.
   The stones are polished.

3. The desert is cleared.
   The stones are put in place.
   The land is measured.
   The stones are polished.
   The pointed stone is set on top.

4. The stones are put in place.
   The pointed stone is set on top.
   The stones are polished.
   The land is measured.
   The desert is cleared.

Which plan do you think is correct?   1   2   3   4

Which plan does your friend think is correct?   1   2   3   4

Which way is correct?

Answer this upside down question, and you will find out.

——————— How many shoes are in a pair?

That is the correct plan number for pyramid building.

22 ▶ Three Poems

Read each poem. Then answer the question below it.

Way Down South

Way down South where bananas grow,
A grasshopper stepped on an elephant's toe.
The elephant said with tears in his eyes,
"Pick on somebody your own size!"

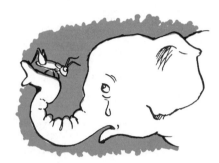

What nonsense is in this poem? _____

_____

As I Was Going Out

As I was going out one day
My head fell off and rolled away.
But when I saw that it was gone,
I picked it up and put it on.

And when I got into the street
A fellow cried: "Look at your feet!"
I looked at them and sadly said:
"I've left them both asleep in bed!"

What is silly in this poem? _____

_____

Hullabaloo

I raised a great hullabaloo
When I found a large mouse in my stew,
  Said the waiter, "Don't shout
  And wave it about,
Or the rest will be wanting one, too!"

Why is this poem funny? _____

_____

Air and Water

This activity is for you to do with an adult.
Read these statements together.

1. Oceans and seas take up about $\frac{2}{3}$ of the earth's surface.
2. The average person uses 168 gallons of water a day.
3. You can live for two weeks without food, two days without water, but only several minutes without air.
4. One molecule out of every 500 molecules of air you breathe has been exhaled by another person.
5. A single car produces more than a ton of harmful gases each year.

Circle the statements you think are true.   1   2   3   4   5

Circle the statements your adult thinks are true.   1   2   3   4   5

Now read the two paragraphs below.
Statements 1, 3, and 5 are true if everything in both paragraphs makes sense.
Statements 2 and 4 are true if everything in one paragraph makes sense but there is nonsense in the other.
All the statements are true if both paragraphs have nonsense.

1. We all need clean air to breathe, but it is hard to keep our air clean. Cars, machines, and factories all create bad gases that dirty the air. Scientists must work hard to find new ways to make our air hard to breathe. Our government has laws telling companies to keep our air as clean as possible. Working together, we can make sure that we always have clean air to breathe.

2. Water pollution is another bad problem. How can we keep our waters polluted and unsafe for fish, people, animals, and plants? Governments all over the world must act together to protect the oceans. Businesses must develop ways to protect our waterways, too. We must all help to keep the water clean.

23 ▸ How I Felt

Remember a time you felt excited.
What happened to make you feel excited?

"I'm so excited!"

_____

_____

_____

Remember a time you laughed.
What happened to make you laugh?

_____

_____

_____

Remember a time you felt surprised.
What happened to make you feel surprised?

_____

_____

_____

Remember a time you felt smart.
What happened to make you feel smart?

_____

_____

_____

Remember a time you felt proud.
What happened to make you feel proud?

_____

_____

_____

What Happened?

Ask a friend to do this activity with you.
Read each story and decide why things happened.
Write your reason.
Then have your friend write a different reason.

Mrs. King opened her refrigerator because she wanted some juice. All the juice was gone. There was nothing left but an empty bottle. Mrs. King was surprised. What could have happened?

My idea _____

_____

My friend's idea _____

_____

Ruth is the best player on the baseball team. Ruth told the coach she could not play in the big game. The coach was surprised. What could have happened?

My idea _____

_____

My friend's idea _____

_____

The Cruz family sat down for dinner. Then, before eating, everyone got up from the table. They left the house, got in the car, and drove to a restaurant. What could have happened?

My idea _____

_____

My friend's idea _____

_____

24 ▸ The Wrong Side

Read this story about a girl named Jody.

The Wrong Side

"Time for breakfast," Jody's mom called.

"I'm coming. Stop rushing me," Jody shouted. She finished combing her hair and picked up her notebook. The book fell and her papers tumbled out. "I hate my notebook. Everything falls out of it."

Jody's mom hurried in to help. "This is easy to fix," she said as she picked up the papers. "There, now everything is in order. Come to breakfast. I made pancakes, your favorite."

"I don't want pancakes," Jody grumbled.

Just then, Jody's baby brother crawled into the room. "Kiss, kiss," he said when he saw his big sister.

"Go away, Ned. I'm busy," Jody shouted.

The little boy began to cry.

"Jody," her mother said, "You certainly got up on the wrong side of the bed this morning."

"What does that mean?" Jody asked.

"It means you are in a bad mood. It means everything is making you angry today."

Jody lay down on her bed. "I'll start today over. This time I'll get up on the right side of the bed."

Pretend Jody woke up in a good mood this morning. Write *two* things that would be different in the story.

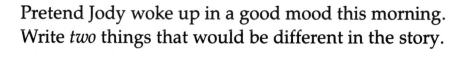

_____

_____

_____

_____

Analyzing a character **49**

Switching Places

Do this activity with an adult.
This part is for you.
Name five things you would do if you were an adult. 1ˢᵗ 2ⁿᵈ 3ʳᵈ 4ᵗʰ 5ᵗʰ

First, I would _____

_____

Second, I would _____

_____

Third, I would _____

_____

Fourth, I would _____

_____

Fifth, I would _____

_____

This part is for your adult.
Name five things you would do if you were a child.

First, I would _____

_____

Second, I would _____

_____

Third, I would _____

_____

Fourth, I would _____

_____

Fifth, I would _____

_____

25 ▸ What's Wrong?

Read this story about Edmund Elf and then study the picture. On the lines below the picture, list six things that are wrong in the picture because they do not match the story.

Edmund Elf lived with his parents, grandparents, and fourteen older brothers and sisters. Edmund hated being the youngest. Everyone bossed him around. He decided to run away from home. Edmund put on his polka dotted shirt and his striped pants. He packed his backpack with his favorite books. Edmund also took his magic ring. With this ring, Edmund could make any wish come true. Then Edmund set off down the road.

Edmund walked until he came to a two story house. Three children were in the yard. They invited Edmund to play. Edmund showed the children his magic ring. The children made wonderful wishes. They wished for a tree house, a cat, and a monkey. Every wish came true. Then the sun began to set. The children begged the little elf to stay and live with them forever. But Edmund was feeling lonely. He missed his mother, his father, and his grandparents. He even missed his brothers and sisters. So Edmund made one more wish that day. Edmund wished to go home.

Things Wrong in the Picture

1. _____

2. _____

3. _____

4. _____

5. _____

6. _____

A Visitor

Do this activity with an adult.
Earth has a visitor.
It is a space traveler from the planet Zygryz.
Here is a description of the Zygryzian.
Read the description aloud to your adult.
Then draw a picture on this page to fit the description.
Have your adult draw a picture on separate paper.
Do not look at each other's drawings until you are finished.
If the adult needs you to reread the description,
you must do it.
When you are finished, compare your drawings.

My Picture of a Zygryzian

The Zygryzian has two orange heads. It has one eye in the middle of each head. It has one antenna on its left head. It has a mouth on the forehead of its left head and a nose on the forehead of its right head. It has long curly yellow hair on its left head and short straight blue hair on its right head. It has two long thin gray necks that meet at a huge fat body. Its body is striped green and purple. It has two pink legs and four red arms with three fingers on each fat hand.

26 Black Holes

You already know information that can help you understand black holes in space.

Write one fact you know about our sun.

_____

Write one fact you know about stars.

_____

Write one fact you know about gravity.

_____

Now read this story about black holes.

When you look at the night sky, you see many stars. The stars look like little bits of light, but that is only because they are so far away. One star is very close to the earth. That star is our sun.

All stars, our sun included, are made of very hot gases. The hot gas moves very fast. Sometimes stars begin to cool. As the stars begin to cool, the gas moves more slowly. Gravity pulls the gases to the center of a star and packs the gases very close together. The star becomes very small and the gases are so close together that no light can escape. That is when a star becomes a black hole.

Gravity from the black hole is so strong that it pulls gases from other stars into its center. The black hole can actually pull neighboring stars apart. Gases in the hole are so close together that one thimbleful weighs billions of tons.

Will our sun ever become a black hole? Maybe, but not for billions and billions of years.

What is one new thing you learned from this story?

_____

Getting to Know You

Do this activity for a friend.
How well do you know your friend?
Fill in the Getting to Know You form.

I didn't know you liked green beans!

Getting to Know You

Write three things your friend does during free time.

1. _____

2. _____

3. _____

Write three animals your friend likes.

1. _____

2. _____

3. _____

Write three things your friend likes to eat.

1. _____

2. _____

3. _____

Write three things your friend would like as gifts.

1. _____

2. _____

3. _____

Read your ideas to your friend.
How many times did your friend agree with your ideas? _____

Name _____

Here are parts of two different story plans.
Each one names the story's characters.
Each one tells where the story takes place, or the **setting**.
Each one gives a problem.
You must think of a way to solve each problem.

PLAN 1

The characters An eight year old girl named Rosa
                    Rosa's grandmother

The setting Grandmother's house late at night

The problem Rosa is living with Grandmother while her
                 parents are away on a trip.
                 Late one night, Grandmother becomes very sick.
                 Grandmother is in her bed and cannot move.
                 She calls for Rosa.

What will Rosa do? _____

_____

_____

PLAN 2

The characters A kind wizard
                    A mean ogre
                    A boy named Carlos

The setting Deep in a forest

The problem The wizard has a magic wand.
                 All of his magic is in the wand.
                 The ogre steals the wand.
                 The wizard asks Carlos to help get the wand back.

What will Carlos do? _____

_____

_____

Spin a Tale

This activity is for you and a friend.
Make number cards like these.

Put the cards face down and mix them up.
Turn over three cards and put them in a row.
The number on the first card tells you which
problem to solve.
Work together with your friend to invent a story to
solve the problem.
Use the character with the same number as the second card.
Use the setting with the same number as the third card.
Take turns adding parts to the story.
Be as silly as you like.
When you are finished, turn over your cards and mix them
up with the rest of the cards.
Then have your friend turn over three cards.
Work together to invent another story.
If the same problem, character, or setting comes up, try
to use it in a different story.
After you finish your second story, decide which story
you both liked better.
On separate paper, draw pictures to go with the story.

Problem	Character	Setting
1. A character is on a sinking ship.	1. a talking cat	1. the beach
2. A character turns invisible.	2. a dragon	2. a science lab
3. A character meets a mean bully.	3. a tiny baby	3. a schoolyard
4. A character is caught in an earthquake.	4. the tooth fairy	4. a mountain top

28 ▶ A True Story

When you study history, you learn about the past.
You learn about events and people from another time.
This story about Lydia Darragh is part of our American history.

In the year 1777, The Americans and the British were
fighting against one another in the American
Revolutionary War. General George Washington was the
leader of the American army. Lydia Darragh was a spy
who helped General Washington.

The British held meetings in Lydia's home. They made
war plans. They did not pay any attention to Lydia, but
that was their mistake.

One night, the British told Lydia they needed her
house for a meeting. Lydia hid in a closet and listened.
She heard the British plan a surprise attack on the
Americans. She knew she had to tell Washington. The
next day, Lydia walked for many hours in the freezing
cold to reach General Washington's troops. She told
them about the attack. Then she walked back home.

Because of Lydia, General Washington was ready
when the British attacked. The British lost the battle.
Thanks to brave Lydia Darragh and many people like
her, the Americans won the Revolutionary War.

Think about Lydia and the kind of person she was.

Write one way you are like Lydia. _____

_____

Write one way you are different from Lydia. _____

_____

If you could talk to Lydia, what would you say to her? _____

_____

Number Tricks

Have a friend do these tricks with you.

Trick 1

Tell your friend to write a number between 1 and 9
on a sheet of paper.
Your friend must not let you see this number or the math
work to come.
Tell your friend to multiply the number by 3.
Next add 2.
Then multiply the new number by 3.
Tell your friend to add the first number to the result.
Your friend should now tell you this final number.
Write the number here.

If your friend did the math correctly, this will be a two
digit number with a 6 in the ones place.
Cross off the 6.
The remaining number is your friend's secret number.

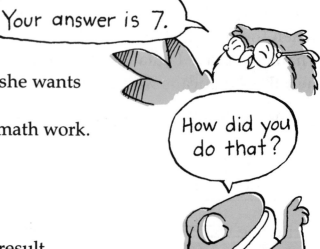

Trick 2

Tell your friend to write any number he or she wants
on a sheet of paper.
You must not see your friend's number or math work.
Tell your friend to add 9 to the number.
Next, double the new number.
Then subtract 4.
Next, divide the new number by 2.
Finally, subtract the first number from the result.
Now, announce to your friend that the number
on his or her page is 7.
If your friend did the math correctly, 7 will always be
the answer.

Name _____

Here is a newspaper story for you to finish.
You may make yourself the star of the story
or you may use any other name you want.
Write all the information needed to tell the news.

A Surprise Winner

Yesterday the town of _____ held its yearly

_____ contest at _____ in the afternoon.

Everyone was surprised when _____ took first place in the

_____ contest. To win the contest _____

had to _____ and _____ and

_____. After the contest, the winner felt _____.

The winner believed this success was due to _____.

The winner said, "_____

_____."

Some of the other contestants felt _____. One of them

said, "_____

_____."

If you want to be in the contest next year, you must _____

_____.

It will also help if you _____

_____.

Story Notes

Play this game with a friend or family member.
Make number cards like these.
Turn the cards face down and mix them up.
Now you will take notes for a newspaper story.
You have to know **who** the story is about, **what** happened,
when it happened, **where** it happened, and **why** it happened.
Take turns picking a card.
The number on the card tells you which box you win from
the News Pool.
Write the information from the box in your Story Notes below.
If you do not need a card, return it face down.
The winner is the first player who completes the story notes.

1	2	3	4
5	6	7	
8	9	10	

News Pool

1 Who	2 What	3 When	4 Where	5 Why
Molly Mouse	spilled the milk	last Monday	in the kitchen	she was looking for cheese
6 Who	**7 What**	**8 When**	**9 Where**	**10 Why**
Karen Cat	had babies	yesterday	in a sock drawer	she wanted a quiet, warm spot

My Story Notes

Who _____

What _____

When _____

Where _____

Why _____

_____

My Friend's Story Notes

Who _____

What _____

When _____

Where _____

Why _____

_____

Name _____

30 ▷ Poem Day

You can write a poem about animals.
Use words from the Word List to finish the sentences.
You may use any other words you want.

Animal Poem

Puppies _____

Cats _____

Fish _____

Birds _____

Hamsters _____

Lions _____

Lambs _____

Monkeys _____

Bears _____.

Word List

scamper	whimper
swish	leap
dive	growl
spin	bubble
soar	flash
purr	stamp
jump	climb
sing	roam
chatter	cuddle
scratch	claw
lick	sniff

Work on a new poem about an imaginary secret pal.
Read all the words in the poem below.
Keep the words that tell about your pal.
Cross out the words that do not tell about your pal.
Add three new words of your own.

My Secret Pal

My pal is
Silly, lively, jumpy, serious,
Jolly, noisy, sneaky, smart,
Flashy, strong, delightful,
Daring, thoughtful, calm,
Polite, sparkly, snuggly,

_____, _____, _____.

A Pocket's Poem

Read this poem to a friend.
When you are finished, fill in your Idea Sheet.
Then have your friend fill in his or her idea sheet.

Keep a Poem in Your Pocket

Keep a poem in your pocket
and a picture in your head
and you'll never feel lonely
at night when you're in bed.

The little poem will sing to you
the little picture bring to you
a dozen dreams to dance to you
at night when you're in bed.

So—
Keep a picture in your pocket
and a poem in your head
and you'll never feel lonely
at night when you're in bed.

Beatrice Schenk de Regniers

My Idea Sheet

Before I go to sleep, I like to _____

_____

_____

At night it would be fun to dream

about _____

_____

_____

My Friend's Idea Sheet

Before I go to sleep, I like to _____

_____

_____

At night it would be fun to dream

about _____

_____

_____

31 ▸ Trick an Ogre

In the story *Puss In Boots,* a clever cat named Puss
tricks an ogre.
The ogre claims it can turn itself into any animal on earth.
Puss asks, "Can you turn yourself into a lion?"
The ogre laughs and turns into the king of beasts.
Then Puss asks, "Can you turn yourself into an elephant?"
The ogre laughs and turns into the huge animal.
Puss says, "You can turn yourself into the biggest of
creatures, but can you turn yourself into a tiny mouse?"
The ogre says, "Of course I can, just watch."
As soon as the ogre turns into a mouse, Puss leaps
on it and eats it up.

How would you trick an ogre?
Choose an idea from the Problem Box or use your own idea.
On the lines below, write a story about how you would solve
the problem by tricking the ogre.

Problem Box

The ogre doesn't want to let you pass its home.

The ogre won't let you have a drink of water from its well.

You need food, but the ogre won't share its bread and soup.

_____

_____

_____

_____

_____

_____

That's Impossible

Do this activity with a friend.
In a tall tale, the storyteller boasts about the characters.
Paul Bunyan is a character in a tall tale.
Here are some of the boasts made about him.

Paul Bunyan was bigger than a house.
When he sneezed, he blew birds out of the air.
Paul was so big he carried trees around in his pockets.
When Paul was a baby, he tossed in his sleep and
knocked down a mile of trees.
Paul had a pancake griddle so huge that a crew
of men strapped bacon slabs to their feet
and skated on the griddle to get it greased.

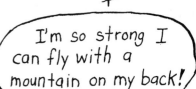

Have a boasting contest with your friend.
Make a huge, fantastic boast about yourself.
Make it a boast that could not possibly be true.
Then challenge your friend to out-boast you.

1. **My Boast**   I am so strong that _____

   _____

   My Friend's Boast   I am so strong that _____

   _____

2. **My Boast**   I am so fast that _____

   _____

   My Friend's Boast   I am so fast that _____

   _____

3. **My Boast**   I hear so well that _____

   _____

   My Friend's Boast   I hear so well that _____

   _____

Enrichment
READING

Grade 3
Answer Key and Teaching Suggestions

AMERICAN EDUCATION PUBLISHING

OVERVIEW

ENRICHMENT READING is designed to provide children with practice in reading and to increase their reading abilities. The program consists of six editions, one each for grades 1 through 6. The major areas of reading instruction—word skills, vocabulary, study skills, comprehension, and literary forms—are covered as appropriate at each level.

ENRICHMENT READING provides a wide range of activities that target a variety of skills in each instructional area. The program is unique because it helps children expand their skills in playful ways with games, puzzles, riddles, contests, and stories. The high-interest activities are informative and fun to do.

Home involvement is important to any child's success in school. *ENRICHMENT READING* is the ideal vehicle for fostering home involvement. Every lesson provides specific opportunities for children to work with a parent, a family member, an adult, or a friend.

AUTHORS

Peggy Kaye, the author of *ENRICHMENT READING*, is also an author of *ENRICHMENT MATH* and the author of two parent/teacher resource books, *Games for Reading* and *Games for Math.* Currently, Ms. Kaye divides her time between writing books and tutoring students in reading and math. She has also taught for ten years in New York City public and private schools.

WRITERS

Timothy J. Baehr is a writer and editor of instructional materials on the elementary, secondary, and college levels. Mr. Baehr has also authored an award-winning column on bicycling and a resource book for writers of educational materials.

Cynthia Benjamin is a writer of reading instructional materials, television scripts, and original stories. Ms. Benjamin has also tutored students in reading at the New York University Reading Institute.

Russell Ginns is a writer and editor of materials for a children's science and nature magazine. Mr. Ginn's speciality is interactive materials, including games, puzzles, and quizzes.

WHY ENRICHMENT READING?

Enrichment and parental involvement are both crucial to children's success in school, and educators recognize the important role work done at home plays in the educational process. Enrichment activities give children opportunities to practice, apply, and expand their reading skills, while encouraging them to think while they read. *ENRICHMENT READING* offers exactly this kind of opportunity. Each lesson focuses on an important reading skill and involves children in active learning. Each lesson will entertain and delight children.

When childen enjoy their lessons and are involved in the activities, they are naturally alert and receptive to learning. They understand more. They remember more. All children enjoy playing games, having contests, and solving puzzles. They like reading interesting stories, amusing stories, jokes, and riddles. Activities such as these get children involved in reading. This is why these kinds of activities form the core of *ENRICHMENT READING.*

Each lesson consists of two parts. Children complete the first part by themselves. The second part is completed together with a family member, an adult, or a friend.

ENRICHMENT READING activities do not require people at home to teach reading. Instead, the activities involve everyone in enjoyable reading games and interesting language experiences.

Published in 1995 by AMERICAN EDUCATION PUBLISHING
© 1991 SRA/McGraw-Hill

HOW TO USE HOMEWORK READING

Each *ENRICHMENT READING* workbook consists of 31 two-page lessons. Each page of a lesson is one assignment. Children complete the first page independently. They complete the second page with a family member, an adult, or a friend. The two pages of a lesson focus on the same reading skill or related skills.

Each workbook is organized into four or five units emphasizing the major areas of reading instruction appropriate to the level of the book. This means you will always have the right lesson available for the curriculum requirements of your child.

The *ENRICHMENT READING* lessons may be completed in any order. They may be used to provide practice at the same time skills are introduced at school, or they may be used to review skills at a later date.

The games and activities in *ENRICHMENT READING* are useful additions to any classroom or home reading program. Beginning on page 68 you will find additional suggestions for classroom games and activities to follow up on the *ENRICHMENT READING* lessons.

Beginning on page 70 you will find the Answer Key for *ENRICHMENT READING*. In many cases, your child's answers will vary according to his or her own thoughts, perceptions, and experiences. Always accept any reasonable answers your child gives.

For exciting activities in mathematics, try . . .

ENRICHMENT MATH

By Peggy Kaye, Carole Greenes, and Linda Schulman

Grades 1 — 6

This delightful program uses a combination of games, puzzles, and activities to extend math skills acquired in the classroom to the real-life world of children and their families. Students using *Enrichment Math* will not be bored by the usual drill-and-practice exercises—they will actually *enjoy* doing their homework!

- Stimulating home activities reinforce classroom instruction in Number Meaning, Geometry, Measurement, and Problem Solving.
- Students become involved in active learning through practical applications of the math skills they learn in class.
- Pleasurable cooperative learning experiences foster positive student feelings about math and homework.
- Interaction among students and parents or other adults is encouraged throughout the program.
- *Enrichment Math* was written by three educators who know math and how children learn.

TEACHING SUGGESTIONS
Grade 3
Optional Activities

A TIP FOR SUCCESS

Children using Grade 3 of *ENRICHMENT READING* will find the games and activities easy to understand and fun to complete. It is a good idea, however, to take a few minutes to explain the assignments. You might also try doing some of the activities and playing some of the games. When children are familiar with the directions and know what is expected of them, they are more likely to complete their work successfully, and the games and activities will add some playful learning to children's reading experiences.

Word Skills

The Word Skills unit contains seven lessons which cover basic decoding skills. Included are lessons on consonants, vowels, syllabication, word endings, compound words, and contractions.

The first three lessons deal with consonant and vowel sounds. You may use the first lesson to provide your child with practice in both short and long vowels. The second lesson concentrates on vowel diphthongs and digraphs, while the third lesson focuses on consonant blends and digraphs. The second page of each lesson is a game. The games will enable you to assign enjoyable word skills practice all year long.

By the time children are using Grade 3, their reading materials often require them to read long words. Children who are able to break words into syllables usually have an easier time sounding out longer words. The activities in Lesson 4 provide children with playful ways to practice their syllabication skills.

Many young children have difficulty with the various plural endings and inflectional endings for words. Two imaginative activities, a drawing activity and an activity with information about bees, and two games will help you provide your child with practice in using these word skills. If your child enjoys playing *Color Three* (page 12) and *Word Collector* (page 14), you may wish to create new game boards with new words for your child to use at home. You might also encourage your child to make his or her own game boards. Help your child research the words and make the game boards.

Study Skills

The Study Skills unit contains two lessons covering dictionary skills. Although children Grade Level 3 will have had some experience using a dictionary, this is also the time when more direct instruction in how to use a dictionary begins.

A full understanding of alphabetical order is crucial to developing good dictionary skills, but many children are bored by exercises that merely ask them to alphabetize words. Lesson 8 takes the boredom away. Most children love to do dot-to-dot drawings, and when words replace the numbers, children enjoy the activity just as much. After your child completes *Follow the Alphabet* (page 17), you may want to adapt some ready-made dot-to-dot drawings by substituting alphabetized words for the numbers.

Children will especially enjoy *Alphabet Code* (page 18) because codes intrigue them. You can make up any number of variations on this activity. Try having children engage in a code speed contest. Call out a word and have children race to put the word into alphabetical order code. The first child to finish says, "Code cracker." Then he or she writes the coded word on the chalkboard. If everyone agrees the word has been properly coded, the child gets one point.

Another important dictionary skill involves becoming familiar with dictionary entries. *Dictionary Mystery* (page 19) and *Dictionary Numbers* (page 20) provide practice with this skill. Here is a variation on *Dictionary Numbers* to use with groups of four children. Give each child four blank cards on which to write dictionary entries. Have each child write an entry word on one card, the pronunciation on another card, a definition on another card, and a sample sentence on the last card. Encourage children to look in the dictionary when making their cards, and provide help as needed. When the children are finished, collect all the cards and shuffle them together. Then deal four cards to each player. Say "Go," and have each player pass one card to the player on the right. Now everyone has a new hand of cards. Let the players inspect their cards, and if one player has a complete dictionary entry, she or he wins the game. If no one has a complete entry, say "Go" again, and have the players pass along another card. Children should continue playing until one player comes up with a complete entry and wins the game.

Vocabulary

The Vocabulary unit contains seven lessons designed to help children develop their vocabularies and increase their general word knowledge. The first lesson focuses on antonyms and synonyms. After completing *An Opposites Poem* (page 21), children may enjoy having an "opposites half hour" at home. During the opposite half hour, whoever speaks should try to say the opposite of what he or she really means. For example, you might say, "Do not get out your notebooks." This translates into "Get out your notebooks." Here is a harder opposite: "Thank you, no one stand up later." This translates into "Please, everyone sit down now." It may be tough living in an opposites world, but it can also be fun.

The second vocabulary lesson deals with homophones. After children complete *Riddle Time* (page 24), you may want to start a homophone riddle collection. Homophone riddles also make good material for handwriting practice. Handwriting lessons are more fun when a funny joke comes into play.

In Lesson 12, children practice using multiple meaning words. You may extend this lesson with the following game. Divide children into teams. Then think of a word with multiple meanings, such as *trip*. Do not tell the children the word. Instead, give two definitions, such as "to stumble" and "a journey," and have the teams try to guess the word. The first team to figure out the word scores one point. If everyone is stumped, give a context sentence using the definitions, such as, "I took a journey to the North Pole and stumbled upon a polar bear." Then let the teams try again to guess the word.

When skillful readers come across unknown words, they can often figure out the meaning of the words from how they are used in the text. To do this, children need to become adept at using context clues. *The Wrong Words* (page 27) and *What's Next?* (page 28) provide children with playful practice in using context clues. To extend these activities, you might try this game. Select a short piece of writing with good context clues. Make a copy and cross out or blank out words in the story that can be figured out from the context. Then make copies for the children and challenge them to replace the words. Each student gets one point for every word she or he replaces correctly. The child or children with the most points wins.

This Leads to That (page 31) and *Shared Thinking* (page 32) give children opportunities to make simple semantic maps. After children complete the activities, encourage them to share their word lists. You may all be surprised by how many different words are included.

Comprehension

The Comprehension unit contains eleven lessons covering all the aspects of comprehension appropriate to Grade 3. The main goal of the games and activities is to help children become actively engaged in reading. You can help by talking about the lessons with your child. When children have opportunities to talk about their work, they feel that their thoughts are important.

To begin, children get practice in finding main ideas and supporting details and in following directions. If your child particularly enjoys *Do As I Say* (page 38), he or she may also enjoy making up his or her own sets of directions and playing the game with others.

Some of the games and activities focus on evaluation and higher order thinking skills, and several of them encourage children to use their imaginations to come up with original responses to open-ended questions. After children complete *Whose Restaurant?* (page 39), encourage them to share their answers. Children may then enjoy making one or more of the dishes listed on the menus, including the specials they added. For the Monster Cafe, children can make the foods out of craft materials. For the two other restaurants, simple recipes can be found and prepared by one child or a group of children. Children may also enjoy playing *Spin a Tale* (page 56). Encourage children to add their own problems, characters, and settings to the lists in order to increase the story possibilities. Make sure children also make additional number cards for the items added to the lists.

Several lessons contain scientific or historical information. If children express particular interest in pyramids, ecology, black holes, giraffes, or elephants, be sure to encourage them to explore these subjects further. There are many appropriate level books on these subjects in libraries and bookstores.

Forms of Writing

The Forms of Writing unit contains four lessons that help children develop appreciation for several different forms of written material. The areas covered are history, mathematics, newspapers, poetry, fairy tales, and tall tales.

After completing *Number Tricks* (page 58), your child may want to do the tricks several times to make sure they work every time.

Before you assign *Poem Day* (page 61), make sure your child understands that not all poems rhyme. In *A Pocket's Poem* (page 62), children have the opportunity to read a delightful poem. They may also enjoy memorizing the poem and reciting it or acting it out in class.

After children complete *That's Impossible* (page 64), they may enjoy drawing pictures to illustrate their favorite boasts. They will also most likely want to have more boasting contests with their friends and family members. This interest can be taken advantage of by exposing children to a variety of tall tales and having them identify the exaggerated and unbelievable elements.

Answer Key
Grade 3–Enrichment Reading

Page 3 1. kite 2. boat 3. pen 4. leaf 5. cane 6. pot 7. rip 8. nail 9. tie 10. hat 11. rose 12. beet; A cricket hears with its legs.

Page 4 Results will vary.

Page 5 *Possible words:* bow, cow, how, low, mow, now, row, tow, vow, clown, down, frown, gown, town; boy, joy, toy, loyal, royal; coin, join, boil, coil, foil, soil; blouse, house, mouse, aloud, cloud, loud, proud

Page 6 Words will vary.

Page 7 *Circled words:* crisp, crust, dream, drip, free, lamp, paint, silk, sweet, swing

Page 8 Words will vary.

Page 9 Names will vary.

Page 10 Results will vary.

Page 11 1. chairs 2. peaches 3. leaves 4. berries 5. bodies; answers will vary

Page 12 *Top row:* shelves, daisies, slices *Middle row:* elbows, ashes, children *Bottom row:* bakeries, tasks, speeches

Page 13 *Lines connect:* shine–shines–shining, gleam–gleams–gleaming, glow–glows–glowing, fly–flies–flying, blaze–blazed–blazing

Page 14 Results will vary.

Page 15 Words and pictures will vary.

Page 16 *Lines between:* we've–we have, it'll–it will, who's–who is, doesn't–does not, you've–you have, wouldn't–would not, you're–you are, you'd–you would, won't–will not

Page 17 a fish

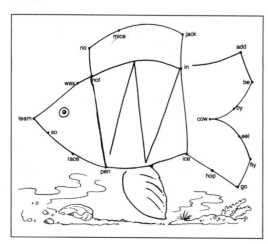

Page 18 Words will vary.

Page 19 *Entry words:* rose, rabbit, fox, piano, lake, baseball

Page 20 Results will vary.

Page 21 *Changed words:* beautiful–ugly, everyone–no one or nobody, sweet–sour, boys–girls, walk–run, backwards–forwards, whisper–shout or yell, girls–boys, big–little or small, long–short, never–always, remember–forget, won't–will, come–leave or go, here–there, out–in; answers will vary

Page 22 Results will vary.

Page 23 here, blew, see, tail, won, new, weigh, waist; 20 + 25 + 25 + 15 + 30 + 25 + 20 + 15 = 175; 175

Page 24 Answers will vary.

Page 25

Page 26 Answers will vary.

Page 27 Your heart beats one hundred thousand times every day!

Page 28 Results will vary.

Page 29 Names will vary.

Page 30 Stories and pictures will vary.

Page 31 Words and sentences will vary.

Page 32 Words and results will vary.

Page 33 *Lines between:* Red is to stop–as green is to go. Car is to road–as train is to track. Hit is to baseball–as kick is to football. Read is to book–as listen is to radio. Apple is to tree–as eggs are to hens.; cat

Page 34 paper, foot, winter, rink, bowl, hot, milk, electricity, lane, button; results will vary

Page 35 Kana; There are many kinds of lava rocks.

Page 36 *My Main Idea:* 2, 3, 6, 8 *My Friend's Main Idea:* 1, 4, 5, 7

Page 37 KEEP UP THE GOOD WORK

Page 38 Results and names will vary.

Page 39 *Left menu:* Baby Bits *Right menu:* Monster Cafe *Bottom menu:* Fitness Food *Today's specials:* answers will vary

Page 40 Answers and results will vary.

Page 41 Answers will vary, but should mention something about the pliers.

Page 42 Answers will vary.

Page 43 1. 7:50 2. red 3. Bugs and Stan 4. eating dinner 5. Stan was at a birthday party 6. Lou 7. robbing Mrs. Glow 8. Lou

Page 44 Plan 2 is in correct order; 2

Page 45 Answers will vary.

Page 46 All the statements are true.

Page 47 Answers will vary.

Page 48 Ideas will vary, but should indicate possible causes of the events.

Page 49 Answers will vary, but should tell two positive things that would be different in the story.

Page 50 Answers will vary.

Page 51 *Things wrong in picture:* dotted pants, striped shirt, five children, three-story house, wand, suitcase

Page 52 Pictures will vary, but should match the description in the story.

Page 53 Answers will vary.

Page 54 Answers will vary.

Page 55 *Plan 1:* Answers will vary, but should tell how Rosa will help Grandmother. *Plan 2:* Answers will vary, but should tell how Carlos will help the wizard get back the wand.

Page 56 Stories and pictures will vary.

Page 57 Answers will vary.

Page 58 *Trick 1:* numbers will vary *Trick 2:* 7

Page 59 Stories will vary, but answers should be appropriate to the context of the story.

Page 60 Answers will vary.

Page 61 Poems will vary.

Page 62 Ideas will vary.

Page 63 Stories will vary, but should tell how to trick an ogre.

Page 64 Boasts will vary.

Also available from American Education Publishing—

MASTER SKILLS SERIES SKILL BOOKS

The Master Skills Series is not just another workbook series. These full-color workbooks were designed by experts who understand the value of reinforcing basic skills! Subjects include Reading, Math, English, Comprehension, Spelling and Writing, and Thinking Skills.

• 88 pages   • 40 titles   • All-color   • $5.95 each

Also Available from American Education Publishing—

BRIGHTER CHILD™ SOFTWARE

The Brighter Child™ Software series is a set of innovative programs designed to teach basic reading, phonics, and math skills in a fun and engaging way to children ages 3 - 9.

Muppet™/Brighter Child™ Software available on CD-ROM

*Same & Different	Sorting & Ordering
*Letters: Capital & Small	Thinking Skills
*Beginning Sounds: Phonics	Sound Patterns: More Phonics

also available on diskette

Brighter Child™ Software available on CD-ROM and diskette

Math Grade 1	Math Grade 2	Math Grade 3
Reading Grade 1	Reading Grade 2	Reading Grade 3

•**call (800) 542-7833 for more information**

Brighter Child™ Software Available at Stores Near You